Take a Stand!®

Modern World History

Reading, Discussing, and Writing

by John De Gree

The Classical Historian
San Clemente, California

DEDICATION

Dedicated to students willing to take a stand

Copyright © 2006 by John De Gree. All rights reserved
Painting by Fran Johnston, Used with permission, © 2006 by John De Gree. All rights reserved
Edited by Laura Vasquez.
Published by The Classical Historian, San Clemente, California 92673.

No part of this work may be reproduced or transmitted in any form or by any means, electronic or mechanical, including photocopying and recording, or by any information storage or retrieval system without the prior written permission of the publisher. Address inquiries to Take a Stand Publications, 1019 Domador, San Clemente, CA 92673. www.takeastandbooks.com

Table of Contents

Part One: Social Studies Curriculum

Chapter I: Social Studies Essay Questions and Prewriting Activities

1. Western Political Thought — 1
2. The Age of Revolution — 6
3. The Age of Napoleon — 11
4. The Industrial Revolution — 16
5. The Age of Imperialism — 21
6. Causes of World War I — 27
7. Effects of World War I — 31
8. The Rise of Totalitarianism — 35
9. World War II—Causes of Appeasement — 40
10. The Cold War in Europe, 1945–1960 — 44
11. The Cold War in Asia, Africa, and Latin America, 1945-1980 — 49
12. Create Your Own Assignment — 54

Part Two: Social Studies Literacy Curriculum

Chapter II: Skills for a One-Paragraph Essay — 55

1. Fact or Opinion? — 55
2. Judgment — 57
3. Supporting Evidence — 58
4. Primary or Secondary Source Analysis — 59
5. Using Quotes — 60
6. Paraphrasing — 61
7. Thesis Statement — 62
8. Conclusion — 63
9. Outline for a One-Paragraph Essay — 64
   Outline Forms for a One-Paragraph Essay — 65
10. Rough Draft for a One-Paragraph Essay — 66
    Rough Draft Forms for a One-Paragraph Essay — 66

Copyright © by John De Gree 2006. All rights reserved

Chapter III: Skills for a Five-Paragraph Essay _____68
    11.   Taking Notes _____68
    12.   Thesis Statement for a Five-Paragraph Essay_____69
    13.   The Topic Sentence and the Closer_____70
    14.   Outlining a Five-Paragraph Essay_____71
           Outline Forms for a Five-Paragraph Essay_____72
    15.   Writing a Rough Draft for a Five-Paragraph Essay_____74
           Rough Draft Forms for a Five-Paragraph Essay_____75
    16.   Revising_____77
    17.   Documenting Sources in the Text_____78
    18.   Works Cited_____79
    19.   Typing Guidelines_____80
    20.   The Cover Page and Checklist_____80

Chapter IV: Skills for a Multi-Page Essay _____81
    21.   Thesis Statement for a Multi-Page Essay_____81
    22.   Counterargument_____82
    23.   Analyzing Primary Sources_____83
    24.   Cause and Effect_____84
    25.   Compare and Contrast_____85
    26.   Outline and Rough Draft for a Multi-Page Essay_____86
           Outline and Rough Draft Forms for a Multi-Page Essay_____87

Chapter V: Grading Rubrics _____91
           One-Paragraph Essay Grading Rubric_____91
           Five-Paragraph Essay Grading Rubric_____92
           Multi-Page Essay Grading Rubric_____93

Part One: Social Studies Curriculum

Chapter I: Social Studies Essay Questions and Prewriting Activities

1. Western Political Thought

The political and legal worlds of ancient Greece and Rome, and the religions of Judaism and Christianity, are commonly considered the beginnings of Western political thought. It is from these lands and religions that much of the western world received the ideas of government, law, philosophy, morality, and religion. Europeans who founded the United States were very aware of the fact that western political thought inspired laws, religions, and customs in the new country.

In your essay, support or reject the statement "Western political thought and the societies from which it originated are based on ideas that are detrimental to humanity."

You should be familiar with these terms and people to answer the question:

Athens	Athenian democracy	Plato	suffrage
citizenship	Pericles	Roman Republic	Judeo-Christian
the Ten Commandments		Roman law	equality

the Stoics and "law of nations"

This essay has six assignments:

Assignment	Due Date		Due Date
1. Prewriting Tasks	_____	4. Rough Draft	_____
2. Thesis Statement	_____	5. Final	_____
3. Outline	_____	6. Works Cited	_____

Prewriting Activities for Essay #1
A. Views of Law and Religion
Judeo-Christian Views of Law and Religion

1. According to the Ten Commandments, are there different rules for the rich and the poor? _____

2. According to the Ten Commandments, did kings have to follow the same rules as servants? _____

3. Based on the teachings of Christianity, is salvation open to everyone, regardless of financial position or race? _____

4. According to Judaism and Christianity, do all people have to follow the same laws of God, or do some people not have to follow them? _____

5. In Judaism and Christianity, are believers in God treated equally, or are there different rules for different people? _____

6. Did Jews and Christians believe in one God, or many gods? _____

7. Did Jews and Christians believe their God had a moral code that humans should follow? _____

8. In which American documents is *equality* referred to? _____

Greco-Roman Views of Law

1. In ancient Athens, did all citizens have the same political rights? _____

2. In the Roman Republic, did all citizens have the same rights? _____

3. In the Roman Republic, what were the Twelve Tables? _____

4. What was similar in the ancient Greek and Roman Republic views of law? _____

5. Were laws in ancient Greece or the Roman Republic written? _____

6. Who were the Stoics of the Roman Republic? _____

7. Who introduced Stoicism in Ancient Athens? _____

8. According to the Stoics, should a society view all people as equals, or should some people have more rights? _____

9. What were the *Twelve Tables* in Roman law? _____

10. In what American documents is *equality* referred to? _____

B. Greco-Roman Traditions of Government

While both Greek and Roman governments had periods of dictatorship, they both also had the world's first elements of democracy. In this exercise, write how democratic Greece and republican Rome functioned.

Athenian Democracy

Five Branches of Government

| Assembly | Council | Board of Generals | Board of Officials | Juries |

1. Briefly list the duties of each of these branches.
   Assembly: _____
   Council: _____
   Board of Generals: _____
   Board of Officials: _____
   Juries: _____

2. In Athens, democracy reached its high point under Pericles (461–429 B.C.). Who could vote during this time? _____
_____

3. Was there another government in the world where people voted for its leader? If so, where? _____

The Roman Republic

Three Branches of Government

| Executive Branch: Two Consuls | Lawmakers: 1. The Senate 2. The Assembly of Tribes 3. The Assembly of Centuries | Judges: Praetors |

1. Which modern country has three branches? _____
_____
2. Why did the Romans think it a good idea to have power in different groups of men? __
_____
_____

C. Summary of Western Political Thought

1. What are a few basic ideas of Western political thought? _____
_____
_____
_____
_____

2. Where did these ideas originate? _____
_____
_____
_____
_____

3. In what countries or societies do we see Western political thought today, and how do we see these ideas in practice? _____
_____
_____
_____
_____

4. Are the ideas of Western political thought exclusive to one ethnic or racial group? For example, are Western political ideas only good for Greeks (as Plato was Greek) or Jews (as Moses was Hebrew)? _____
Explain your answer. _____
_____
_____

5. Are the ideas of Western political thought too hard for today's student to understand? Were people a few thousand years ago more intelligent than we are today? _____
_____
_____
_____

D. Class Discussion

When you share ideas with other students, your ideas may be reinforced, rejected, or slightly changed. Listening to your classmates' ideas will help you form your own judgment.

Each student must interview at least three classmates who do not sit next to one another. The answers to the following questions must be written down on a piece of paper.

1. What is your name?
2. Are western political thought and the societies from which it originated based on ideas that are detrimental to the human race?
3. Which facts do you have that support what you think?

Reflection

After you have written down all your classmates' responses, think about them and ask yourself the following questions. Write down your answers under your classmates' responses.

1. What do I think of my classmates' answers?
2. Which questions are the best to questions #2 above?
3. Have I changed the way I think? How?

You should now have a chance to present your ideas in a class discussion. If somebody says something with which you disagree, speak up! In your discussion, you may find out they are actually right and you are wrong. All possible viewpoints should be stated and defended out loud. Test your ideas in class.

2. The Age of Revolution

For most of the medieval ages (c. A.D. 476–1500), Europeans did not question the divine right of kings and queens. Europeans believed that God personally chose their leaders, and therefore following the rulers was both a political and a religious act. In some lands the king exercised absolute power, that is, power without limits.

From the 1600s through the mid 1800s, however, revolution swept through many of the great countries of Europe and its large colonies. Kings were violently deposed from power, in some cases losing their heads in public executions. The era of divine right was forever broken, and the age of revolution heralded new ideologies.

In your essay, answer the question "What was the key factor in destroying the idea of the divine right of kings?" Explain what ended the power of the great absolute monarchs and brought in a radically different kind of state.

As you write your essay, you should be familiar with the following ideas and terms:

nationalism	absolute monarch	limited monarchy
Enlightenment	self-government	English Bill of Rights
Magna Carta	Declaration of Independence	

This essay has six assignments:

Assignment	Due Date		Due Date
1. Prewriting Tasks	_____	4. Rough Draft	_____
2. Thesis Statement	_____	5. Final	_____
3. Outline	_____	6. Works Cited	_____

Prewriting Activities for Essay #2
A. Important Documents on the Rights of the Individual

Research the following documents and provide a short summary for each. Then answer the questions at the bottom of the page.

The Magna Carta (1215): _____   _____   _____
The English Bill of Rights (1689): _____   _____   _____
The American Declaration of Independence (1776): _____   _____   _____
The French Declaration of the Rights of Man and the Citizen (1789): _____   _____   _____
The American Bill of Rights (1791): _____   _____   _____

Questions
1. Did these documents grant more power to the king (or government), or less? _____   _____
2. Which of the documents guarantees the most individual freedom from government? ___   _____

Copyright © by John De Gree 2006. All rights reserved

B. The Enlightenment

Research these philosophers of the Enlightenment and write down their main ideas involving the ideas of good government.

Political Philosophers
John Locke: _____ _____ _____ _____
Thomas Hobbes: _____ _____ _____ _____
Charles Louis-Montesquieu: _____ _____ _____ _____
Jean-Jacque Rousseau: _____ _____ _____ _____

Economics and the Enlightenment
Research the following economic term and its most known proponent.
Laissez faire: _____ _____ _____
Adam Smith: _____ _____ _____

Questions
1. Did the philosophers of the Enlightenment want a stronger King? _____ _____
2. Do you think that most kings were in favor of or against philosophers of the Enlightenment? Why or why not? _____ _____

C. Nationalism

1. What is nationalism? _____
_____

2. When did the idea of nationalism become a major factor in European politics? ___
_____

3. How did Napoleon Bonaparte spread ideas of nationalism in Europe? _____
_____

4. Did the idea of nationalism support having empires controlled by a king from a different nationality? _____
_____

5. In England, under King Henry VIII, what did the British king do to the Roman Catholic Church? _____
_____

6. In the German speaking lands, during the life of Martin Luther, describe what was happening in Europe. _____
_____

7. Did the Protestant Reformation support the idea of divine right, or weaken it? ___
_____

8. Did the idea of nationalism make kings of multinational countries stronger, or weaker? Why? _____
_____

D. Class Discussion

When you share ideas with other students, your ideas may be reinforced, rejected, or slightly changed. Listening to your classmates' ideas will help you form your own judgment.

Each student must interview at least three classmates who do not sit next to one another. The answers to the following questions must be written down on a piece of paper.

1. What is your name?
2. What was the key factor in destroying the idea of the divine right of Kings?
3. How did you find your answers?

Reflection

After you have written down all your classmates' responses, think about them and ask yourself the following questions. Write down your answers under your classmates' responses.

1. What do I think of my classmates' answers?
2. Which answer to question #2 above was the best?
3. Have I changed the way I think?
4. How have I changed the way I think?

You should now have a chance to present your ideas in a class discussion. If somebody says something with which you disagree, speak up! In your discussion, you may find out they are actually right and you are wrong. All possible viewpoints should be stated and defended out loud. Test your ideas in class.

3. The Age of Napoleon

Napoleon Bonaparte was born and raised on the French-controlled island Corsica. Of lower nobility, Napoleon went to France at the age of 13 to learn how to become a soldier. As a young man and officer in the army, France was in thralls to the French Revolution and the Reign of Terror. During this time, over 40,000 Frenchmen were executed and chaos ruled in France. Peasant revolts swept the countryside and European empires invaded France in an attempt to restore the king. Searching for order and stability, the French turned to Napoleon, who quickly rose to power through his military prowess. Napoleon used the power of the military and his charisma to take over France.

Once in charge of France, Napoleon took the ideals of the French Revolution and brought them to the rest of Europe. The French Revolution was, in part, an attempt to bring great reforms in society. These changes meant to rid Europe of slavery and inequality. By military conquest Napoleon introduced these liberal ideas to the rest of Europe. On one hand, Napoleon promoted the freeing of slaves, suffrage for adult males, and the dissolution of empires that may have discriminated against ethnic minorities. On the other hand, Bonaparte militarily conquered nearly all of Europe, destroying armies and empires and forcing nations either to be part of France or to be its ally.

In your essay, discuss the accomplishments and failures of Napoleon and take a stand on this question "Was Napoleon a hero or a villain?" Use sound evidence and logical arguments to defend your thesis.

Be familiar with these terms:

nationalism	the French Revolution	the Enlightenment
empire	constitutional monarchy	Napoleonic Code
Declaration of the Rights of Man	Jacobins	Reign of Terror
King Louis XVI	Napoleonic Wars	

This essay has six assignments:

Assignment	Due Date		Due Date
1. Prewriting Tasks	_____	4. Rough Draft	_____
2. Thesis Statement	_____	5. Final	_____
3. Outline	_____	6. Works Cited	_____

Prewriting Activities for Essay #3
A. The French Revolution

1. In 1788 France…..
    a. Who was the First Estate?_____
    _____
    b. Who was the Second Estate?_____
    _____
    c. Who was the Third Estate?_____
    _____
    d. Which two estates ruled but represented a small number of French?_____
    _____

2. In 1788 France, did the law treat everyone the same? Did a poor person have the same rights as the king? _____
_____

3. A society where some people have more rights than others is a society of _____

4. Who created the National Assembly and why?_____
_____

5. What happened on July 14, 1789, at the Bastille? Why? _____
_____
_____

6. What did the Declaration of the Rights of Man state? _____
_____
_____

7. Why did Prussia, Austria, and later Britain, Spain, and Holland all attack France? ____
_____

8. Who were the Jacobins and the Committee on Public Safety? _____
_____

9. What happened to King Louis XVI and his wife, Queen Marie Antoinette? _____

10. In the Reign of Terror, what was life like in France (How many died? Why were they killed? Who was Robespierre)? _____
_____
_____

11. What military leader ended the French Revolution? _____
_____
_____

B. The Age of Napoleon

I. **The Napoleonic Code:** Once in power, Napoleon ended the French Revolution and the Reign of Terror. Stability and order returned to France. Napoleon created a new set of laws for France, known as the *Code Napoleon*, or the *Napoleonic Code*. This code is still the basis for law in France. Under the code, slaves were freed, and a more equal society was created.

   A. What does this code say about equality of citizens under the law? _____

   B. How does the code deal with religion? _____

   C. How was the Napoleonic Code different from law under the king? _____

   D. What is a plebiscite and for whom did the French vote a plebiscite for? _____

   E. Do you think the Napoleonic Code was good for France? Why or why not? _____

   F. The Napoleonic Code has been used in many countries, and even in some states in the U.S.A. (such as Louisiana). Did Napoleon positively affect society where his code was adopted? Why or why not? _____

II. **The Napoleonic Wars (1805-1815):** Although under Napoleon stability and order returned, peace did not. France tirelessly waged war on all of Europe.

   A. Napoleon crowned himself the emperor of France. Why didn't he let the Pope crown him? _____

   B. Name the kingdoms that Napoleon conquered. _____

   C. What was the *Continental System*? _____

   D. What revolutionary ideas did the French spread when Napoleon conquered other lands? _____

   E. How did Spain react after Napoleon's invasion? _____

   F. What invasion by Napoleon began his downfall? _____

   G. Which battle was Napoleon's last? _____

C. Quotations on the Age of Napoleon

Read the following quotes from Napoleon Bonaparte and briefly describe — based on his words what type of person he was.

"It is the cause, not the death, that makes the martyr."
"Never interrupt your enemy when he is making a mistake."
"Victory belongs to the most persevering."
"Take time to deliberate, but when the time for action has arrived, stop thinking and go on."
"I have fought sixty battles and I have learned nothing which I did not know at the beginning."
"A Constitution should be short and obscure."
"Death is nothing, but to live defeated and inglorious is to die daily."
"If I had to choose a religion, the sun as the universal giver of life would be my god."
"In order to govern, the question is not to follow out a more or less valid theory but to build with whatever materials are at hand. The inevitable must be accepted and turned to advantage."

_____
_____
_____
_____
_____
_____
_____
_____
_____
_____
_____
_____
_____
_____
_____
_____

D. Class Discussion

When you share ideas with other students, your ideas may be reinforced, rejected, or slightly changed. Listening to your classmates' ideas will help you form your own judgment.

Each student must interview at least three classmates who do not sit next to one another. The answers to the following questions must be written down on a piece of paper.

1. What is your name?
2. Was Napoleon a hero or a villain?
3. What is your supporting evidence?

Reflection

After you have written down all your classmates' responses, think about them and ask yourself the following questions. Write down your answers under your classmates' responses.

1. What do I think of my classmates' answers?
2. Which are the best three answers to question #2 above?
3. Have I changed the way I think?
4. How have I changed the way I think?

You should now have a chance to present your ideas in a class discussion. If somebody says something with which you disagree, speak up! In your discussion, you may find out they are actually right and you are wrong. All possible viewpoints should be stated and defended out loud. Test your ideas in class.

4. The Industrial Revolution

The Industrial Revolution in Western Europe and the United States took place roughly between 1750 and 1900. It is called a revolution because of the dramatic change that took place in people's daily lives. In manufacturing, science, transportation, communication, and the workplace, inventions, discoveries, and new ideas altered how people viewed the world and how they lived.

In your essay, discuss the most important changes to society during the Industrial Revolution. In what field did inventions or discoveries cause the greatest change in the everyday life of humans? You may choose from the following list: science, medicine, transportation, agriculture, manufacturing, and communication.

You should be familiar with advances and changes in these areas between 1750 and 1900:

medicine   science   transportation   agriculture

manufacturing   communication   philosophy

This essay has six assignments:

Assignment	Due Date		Due Date
1. Prewriting Tasks	_____	4. Rough Draft	_____
2. Thesis Statement	_____	5. Final	_____
3. Outline	_____	6. Works Cited	_____

Prewriting Activities for Essay #4
A. The Industrial Revolution

Research the greatest changes of the Industrial Revolution in the following categories.

MEDICINE		
Person	**Invention or discovery**	**Effect on society**
Edward Jenner		
	Pasteurization	Drinking was safer
Robert Koch		
	Antiseptics	Killed germs and made operating cleaner and safer

SCIENCE		
Person	**Invention or discovery**	**Effect on society**
John Dalton	Atoms	
Michael Faraday		
	X ray	Doctors could look inside the body without operating
Marie Curie	Radioactive elements: radium and polonium	

TRANSPORTATION		
Person	**Invention or discovery**	**Effect on society**
Robert Fulton		Travel time on water was shortened
George Stephens	Train	
Karl Benz		
	Airplane	

AGRICULTURE

Person	Invention/discovery	Effect on society
Jethro Tull	Seed drill	
	Crop rotation	
Cyrus McCormick	Mechanical reaper	
John Deere		It was easier to plow

MANUFACTURING

Person	Invention or discovery	Effect on society
John Kay	Flying shuttle	
James Hargreaves		
	Power loom	
Eli Whitney	Cotton gin	

COMMUNICATION

Person	Invention or discovery	Effect on society
Samuel F.B. Morse		
	Wireless telegraph	
Vladimir Zworyka	Television	

B. Reflection

Look over the notes you've taken on the last two pages. Answer the following questions.

1. Based on your notes, in what field did inventions or discoveries cause the greatest change in the everyday life of humans? _____
_____

2. How did inventions or discoveries in this field effect (change) everyday life? _____
_____
_____
_____
_____

3. In what field did inventions or discoveries cause the second-greatest change in the everyday life of humans? _____
_____

4. How did inventions or discoveries in this field effect (change) everyday life? _____
_____
_____
_____
_____

5. Choose one person you think was most responsible for the greatest advancement made during the Industrial Revolution. What did he or she invent or discover, and how did this greatly impact the everyday life of humans? _____
_____
_____
_____
_____

Copyright © by John De Gree 2006. All rights reserved

C. Class Discussion

When you share ideas with other students, your ideas may be reinforced, rejected, or slightly changed. Listening to your classmates' ideas will help you form your own judgment.

Each student must interview at least three classmates who do not sit next to one another. The answers to the following questions must be written down on a piece of paper.

1. What is your name?
2. In what field did inventions or discoveries cause the greatest change in the everyday life of humans?
3. How did you find your answers?

Reflection

After you have written down all your classmates' responses, think about them and ask yourself the following questions. Write down your answers under your classmates' responses.

1. What do I think of my classmates' answers?
2. Which are the best three answers to question #2 above?
3. Have I changed the way I think?
4. How have I changed the way I think?

You should now have a chance to present your ideas in a class discussion. If somebody says something with which you disagree, speak up! In your discussion, you may find out they are actually right and you are wrong. All possible viewpoints should be stated and defended out loud. Test your ideas in class.

5. The Age of Imperialism

In the nineteenth century, major industrialized European countries and the United States colonized much of Africa, Latin America, and Asia. Because of the organizational and economic strength of the industrialized nations, small countries were able to master populations many times their size. In 1850, Great Britain was able to rule a nation of 150,000,000 with only 34,000 British soldiers. British rule in India began in the 1700s — when the British East India Company began controlling large areas of land — and lasted until 1947.

In your essay, trace British imperialism in India from the onset of colonization to Indian independence. Show the perspectives of the colonizer and the colonized, paying close attention to the role of leaders and religion in the movements for independence. Compare and contrast the different views on British colonization of India.

To write a good essay, you should be familiar with these terms and people:

British East India Company	Sepoy Rebellion	Hindus
Muslims	suttee	nationalism
democracy	famine	racism
Queen Victoria	Mohandas K. Gandhi	passive resistance

This essay has six assignments:

Assignment	Due Date		Due Date
1. Prewriting Tasks	_____	4. Rough Draft	_____
2. Thesis Statement	_____	5. Final	_____
3. Outline	_____	6. Works Cited	_____

Prewriting Activities for Essay #5
A. Taking Notes

When researching, do not look in the index of your textbook. Look in the table of contents for "Imperialism in India," "British Imperialism," or a similar heading. On your own page continue researching the rest of the terms.

British East India Company
What? _____
Who? _____
When? _____
Where? _____
Why? _____
Any other information? _____
_____
Source: _____

The Sepoy Rebellion
What? _____
Who? _____
When? _____
Where? _____
Why? _____
Any other information? _____
_____
Source: _____

Hindus in India
What? _____
Who? _____
When? _____
Where? _____
Why? _____
Any other information? _____
_____
Source: _____

B. The British in India

1. What was the British East India Company and when did it begin to do business in India? _____

2. In the early 1700s, besides Great Britain, what European power did business in India? _____

3. List two reasons the British thought they were better than the Indians? _____

4. Describe the Sepoy Rebellion. _____

5. Describe the practice of suttee. Why did the British outlaw this in India? _____

6. What did the British introduce to India that involved transportation? _____

7. In education and medicine, how did the British influence India? _____

8. When did Queen Victoria become *Empress of India*? _____

9. What was the Indian National Congress? _____

10. What was the Muslim League? _____

11. When did the British leave India and give her independence? _____

12. What countries did the British create from India and why? _____

13. Read the poem on the following page by Rudyard Kipling, an Englishman born and raised in British India. What can we learn from a poem to help us understand history? _____

C. "The White Man's Burden," by Rudyard Kipling (1865-1936)

1. Take up the White Man's burden--
Send forth the best ye breed--
Go, bind your sons to exile
To serve your captives' need;
To wait, in heavy harness,
On fluttered folk and wild--
Your new-caught sullen peoples,
Half devil and half child.

2. Take up the White Man's burden--
In patience to abide,
To veil the threat of terror
And check the show of pride;
By open speech and simple,
An hundred times made plain,
To seek another's profit
And work another's gain.

3. Take up the White Man's burden--
The savage wars of peace--
Fill full the mouth of Famine,
And bid the sickness cease;
And when your goal is nearest
(The end for others sought)
Watch sloth and heathen folly
Bring all your hope to nought.

4. Take up the White Man's burden--
No iron rule of kings,
But toil of ser and sweeper--
The tale of common things,
The ports ye shall not enter,
The roads ye shall not tread,
Go, make them with your living
And mark them with your dead.

5. Take up the White Man's burden,
And reap his old reward--
The blame of those ye better
The hate of those ye guard--
The cry of hosts ye humour
(Ah, slowly!) toward the light:-
"Why brought ye us from bondage,
Our loved Egyptian night?"

6. Take up the White Man's burden--
Ye dare not stoop to less--
Nor call too loud on Freedom
To cloak your weariness,
By all ye will or whisper,
By all ye leave or do,
The silent sullen peoples
Shall weigh your God and you.

7. Take up the White Man's burden!
Have done with childish days--
The lightly-proffered laurel,
The easy ungrudged praise:
Comes now, to search your manhood
Through all the thankless years,
Cold, edged with dear-bought wisdom,
The judgment of your peers.

1. In this poem, how does Kipling view the Indians? _____

2. How does he view the British as colonizers? _____

3. What do the lines "The silent sullen peoples/ Shall weigh your God and you" mean? ___

4. In this poem, is Kipling against British colonization of India or for it? _____

D. Mohandas K. Gandhi (1869-1948)

1. Where was Gandhi born? _____

2. At what age did he marry? _____

3. Where did he study to be a lawyer? _____

4. Gandhi worked in South Africa for many years. What was his work there? _____

5. What does *passive resistance* mean? _____

6. What did Gandhi think about British colonization in India? _____

7. How did Gandhi work to rid India of British occupation? _____

8. What were two major religions of India in the nineteenth century? _____

9. How did people of these two religions get along? _____

10. When did India achieve independence from Great Britain? _____

11. What two countries were created from India and why? _____

12. During his life Gandhi would fast (not eat). What were some reasons for his fasting? _____

13. Gandhi is called *Mohatma* in India. What does this mean and why is he called this? _____

14. From where did Gandhi say he receive his courage? How could he stand up to the British empire without any weapons? _____

15. What role did religion play in the life of Gandhi? _____

16. What major U.S. figure of the twentieth century studied Gandhi and replicated the strategy of nonviolent protest? _____

E. Class Discussion

When you share ideas with other students, your ideas may be reinforced, rejected, or slightly changed. Listening to your classmates' ideas will help you form your own judgment.

Each student must interview at least three classmates who do not sit next to one another. The answers to the following questions must be written down on a piece of paper.

1. What is your name?
2. How did the British view colonization of India?
3. How did the Indians view British colonization of India?
4. Which facts do you have that support your answers?

Reflection

After you have written down all your classmates' responses, think about them and ask yourself the following questions. Write down your answers under your classmates' responses.

1. What do I think of my classmates' answers?
2. Which are the best three answers to questions #2 and #3 above?
3. Have I changed the way I think?
4. How have I changed the way I think?

You should now have a chance to present your ideas in a class discussion. If somebody says something with which you disagree, speak up! In your discussion, you may find out they are actually right and you are wrong. All possible viewpoints should be stated and defended out loud. Test your ideas in class.

6. Causes of World War I

Can the value of one life be so high that it could start a world war? In 1914, Serbian nationalists shot the future ruler of the Austro-Hungarian Empire, Archduke Francis Ferdinand. This one act started a chain reaction, setting off a series of events that led to the first great catastrophic war of the twentieth century. At the time it was called *The War to End All Wars*, or *The Great War*. President Woodrow Wilson had high hopes this war would make the world "safe for democracy." Unfortunately, World War I became Act I of a terrible play for humanity. In addition, many of the European countries that fought in World War I turned to totalitarian governments after the war.

In your essay, discuss and evaluate the causes of World War I. After the Serbs assassinated Archduke Francis Ferdinand, was World War I avoidable? If your research shows you it was avoidable, explain how Europeans could have avoided the death and destruction of this four-year conflict. If you find it was unavoidable, explain your answer.

To answer the question, you should be familiar with these terms and people as they relate to World War I:

nationalism	imperialism	alliances	militarism
balance of power	Pan-Slavism	Pan-Germanism	the Triple Alliance
assassination of Archduke Francis Ferdinand			the Triple Entente
Balkans	First Balkan War	Second Balkan War	

This essay has six assignments:

Assignment	Due Date		Due Date
1. Prewriting Tasks	_____	4. Rough Draft	_____
2. Thesis Statement	_____	5. Final	_____
3. Outline	_____	6. Works Cited	_____

Prewriting Activities for Essay #6
A. Possible Causes of World War I

When researching, do not look in the index of your textbook. Look in the table of contents for "World War I" or for "Causes of World War I." On your own page continue researching the rest of the terms.

Nationalism
What? _____
Who? _____
When? _____
Where? _____
Was this one cause of World War I? How? _____
_____
_____
_____
_____
Source: _____

Imperialism
What? _____
Who? _____
When? _____
Where? _____
Was this one cause of World War I? How? _____
_____
_____
_____
_____
Source: _____

Alliances
What? _____
Who? _____
When? _____
Where? _____
Was this one cause of World War I? How? _____
_____
_____
_____
_____
Source: _____

B. Evaluating Causes

On the chart below, first write all the causes of World War I on the right. (You may have causes that are not found on the assignment page. You may also decide not to use all the terms from the assignment page.) Then rank the causes on the left from 1-10, 1 being the greatest cause and 10 the weakest.

Ranking (1–10)	Causes of World War I

Questions

1. Explain your top three rankings. Why do you think these top three were the greatest causes of World War I? _____
_____
_____
_____
_____
_____
_____

2. After the assassination of Archduke Francis Ferdinand, do you think World War I was avoidable? If so, what could have been done to avoid the war? If you think the war was unavoidable, explain why you think this. _____
_____
_____
_____
_____

C. Class Discussion

When you share ideas with other students, your ideas may be reinforced, rejected, or slightly changed. Listening to your classmates' ideas will help you form your own judgment.

Each student must interview at least three classmates who do not sit next to one another. The answers to the following questions must be written down on a piece of paper.

1. What is your name?
2. Where did you do most of your research?
3. After the Serbs assassinated Archduke Francis Ferdinand, was World War I avoidable? Why or why not?

Reflection

After you have written down all your classmates' responses, think about them and ask yourself the following questions. Write down your answers under your classmates' responses.

1. What do I think of my classmates' answers?
2. Which are the best three answers to question #3 above?
3. Have I changed the way I think?
4. How have I changed the way I think?

You should now have a chance to present your ideas in a class discussion. If somebody says something with which you disagree, speak up! In your discussion, you may find out they are actually right and you are wrong. All possible viewpoints should be stated and defended out loud. Test your ideas in class.

7. Effects of World War I

World War I was a war of incredible and catastrophic scope. This "War to End All Wars" may have caused the Russian Revolution, the rise of Hitler, World War II, and the disillusionment of a generation. For the next 70 years, the effects of World War I could be felt throughout the world. Europe — the continent of Socrates, Euclid, Augustine, Dante, and Aquinas — sparked a war that killed over ten million, wounded over 20 million, and may have led to the enslavement of tens of millions in totalitarian regimes. How could such an advanced culture of countries have created the groundwork for the most violent century of humanity?

In your essay, discuss the various aims of world leaders at the Paris Peace Conference. Based on your research, were Woodrow Wilson's aims at the conference visionary or naïve? In your answer, compare and contrast the aims of the world leaders with Wilson's goals.

To answer your question best, you should be familiar with these terms and people:

David Lloyd George (Britain)	Georges Clemenceau (France)
Vittorio Orlando (Italy)	Woodrow Wilson (U.S.A.)
secret treaties	Fourteen Points
the Treaty of Versailles	definitions of "visionary" and "naïve"

This essay has six assignments:

Assignment	Due Date		Due Date
1. Prewriting Tasks	_____	4. Rough Draft	_____
2. Thesis Statement	_____	5. Final	_____
3. Outline	_____	6. Works Cited	_____

Prewriting Activities for Essay #7
A. Secret Treaties

The winning powers of World War I had created secret treaties among each other to divide up the Central Powers, who had lost the war. According to these treaties, the Ottoman Empire, Germany, and Austria-Hungary were to lose parts of their own territories and at least parts of their colonies. In this section of your prewriting activities, research the secret treaties made by the victorious powers of World War I. The United States, led by President Woodrow Wilson, did not make secret treaties.

Spoils of war is a term that refers, in part, to the property or money that the victors in war receive. Russia, Great Britain, France, and Italy made secret treaties that were to dismember the losing countries.

In the following graph, write what was promised the victors of war.

The Spoils of War: the Secret Treaties		
Country	**Leader in 1919**	**Territory Promised in Secret Treaties if Country Won the War**
1. France	1. Clemenceau	1. Alsace and Lorraine from Germany
		2. Portions of the Ottoman Empire
		3.
		4.
2. Great Britain	2.	1.
		2.
		3.
3. Italy	3.	1.
		2.
		3.
4. Romania	4.	1.
5. Japan	5.	1.
6. Russia	6.	1.
		2.
(Because Russia dropped out of the war (lost to Germany), it could not cash in on its secret peace treaties.)		
7. Serbia	7.	1.

Question
Based on these secret treaties between the World War I victors, describe the aims of these leaders at the Paris Peace Conference. _____
_____
_____
_____

B. Woodrow Wilson's Fourteen Points

When President Woodrow Wilson attended the Paris Peace Conference after World War I, he came with a plan for Europe and the world that he called "the Fourteen Points." In this prewriting activity, research the main ideas of the Fourteen Points, and think how these ideas compare with the secret treaties of the victorious European leaders of World War I.

Main Ideas of Wilson's Fourteen Points	
Main Ideas	Explanation
1. Freedom of the seas	1. The oceans should be open for every country to use without threat of violence.
2. No secret treaties	2.
3. Arms reduction	3.
4. League of nations	4.
5. Self-determination and nationality	5.

Questions

Compare and contrast the secret treaties with Woodrow Wilson's Fourteen Points.

1. Based on these main ideas of Wilson's Fourteen Points, describe this president's aims at the Paris Peace Conference in a sentence or two. _____

2. How did Wilson's aims differ from the other leaders' aims at the Peace Conference? _____

3. Which plan — the secret treaties or Wilson's Fourteen Points — do you think would do more for world peace? Explain. _____

C. Class Discussion

When you share ideas with other students, your ideas may be reinforced, rejected, or slightly changed. Listening to your classmates' ideas will help you form your own judgment.

Each student must interview at least three classmates who do not sit next to one another. The answers to the following questions must be written down on a piece of paper.

1. What is your name?
2. Were U.S. President Woodrow Wilson's Fourteen Points visionary or naïve?
3. How did you find your answers?

Reflection

After you have written down all your classmates' responses, think about them and ask yourself the following questions. Write down your answers under your classmates' responses.

1. What do I think of my classmates' answers?
2. Which are the best three answers to question #2 above?
3. Have I changed the way I think?
4. How have I changed the way I think?

You should now have a chance to present your ideas in a class discussion. If somebody says something with which you disagree, speak up! In your discussion, you may find out they are actually right and you are wrong. All possible viewpoints should be stated and defended out loud. Test your ideas in class.

8. The Rise of Totalitarianism

The period between the end of World War I and the onset of World War II was a time of great instability, world depression, and disillusionment of republican values in the great powers of Germany, Italy, and Russia (Soviet Union). Totalitarian governments emerged in these societies and threatened not only Europe, but the entire world as well. *Fascism* and *communism*, though enemies to each other, were two types of totalitarian systems which shared many traits.

In your essay, trace the origins of fascism and communism. Compare and contrast these two totalitarian regimes in terms of political philosophy, their aggressive nature, and cost in human lives.

You should be familiar with these terms and people as they relate to the rise of totalitarianism:

fascism	communism	world depression (1930s)
totalitarianism	Vladimir Lenin	Josef Stalin
Adolf Hitler	Benito Mussolini	Weimar Republic
human rights	Russian Revolution	Karl Marx

This essay has six assignments:

Assignment	Due Date		Due Date
1. Prewriting Tasks	_____	4. Rough Draft	_____
2. Thesis Statement	_____	5. Final	_____
3. Outline	_____	6. Works Cited	_____

Prewriting Activities for Essay #8
A. Taking Notes

Follow the structure below to write notes:

Fascism

What?_____
Who?_____
When?_____
Where?_____
Why?_____
Any other information? _____
_____
Source:_____

Communism

What?_____
Who?_____
When?_____
Where?_____
Why?_____
Any other information? _____
Source:_____

World Depression

What?_____
Who?_____
When?_____
Where?_____
Why?_____
Any other information? _____
Source:_____

B. The Rise of Communism

1. What are the main points of *The Communist Manifesto* (1848) by Karl Marx and Robert Engels? _____
_____
_____

2. What kind of government did Russia have in 1916? _____
_____

3. What were the problems in Russia in 1916? _____

4. Who were the Bolsheviks and when did they take over Russia? _____
_____

5. In 1920, who were the top two Bolsheviks in Russia? _____

6. Under Vladimir Lenin, Russia reorganized into a federation. What was the new name of the country? _____

7. In the Soviet Union what freedoms were denied? What could people not do, nor say, that they could in the United States? _____
_____

8. What did the Communists do to private property and to Church property? Why? ____
_____

9. After Lenin died who took over in the Soviet Union? _____

10. What was *The Five-Year Plan*? _____

11. How many civilian lives were killed because of communism? _____
_____

12. The Soviet Union is known as the world's first modern totalitarian state. Why was it called totalitarian? _____
_____

13. How long did the Communists remain in power in the Soviet Union? _____

14. In a Communist state, who or what is more important — the state or the individual? _
_____

15. Does communism continue the tradition of Western political thought, begun by the Greco-Roman and Judeo-Christian cultures? How or how not? _____
_____
_____

Copyright © by John De Gree 2006. All rights reserved

C. The Rise of Fascism

1. What problems did Italy have after World War I? _____
_____

2. Who was the leader of the Fascists in Italy and what name did he give himself? _____
_____

3. From whom did the Italian Fascists claim they were protecting Italy? _____
_____

4. How did Mussolini seize power in Italy? _____
_____
_____
_____

5. Who controlled businesses and employees in Fascist Italy? _____
_____

6. What was the Lateran Treaty? _____
_____

7. Who or what was more important in Fascist Italy, the state or the individual? _____
_____

8. After World War I, what economic problems did the first democratically elected government in Germany, the Weimar Republic, have? _____
_____

9. After World War I, which countries occupied parts of Germany? _____
_____

10. Under the Weimar Republic, Germany had to admit *war guilt* for World War I and pay war reparations to the victors of WW I. How did this make Germans feel? _____
_____

11. What was the shorter name for the *National Socialist German Worker's Party* in Germany? _____

12. What is a scapegoat? How did Hitler and the Nazis use the Jews as a scapegoat for Germany's problems? _____
_____

13. What did Hitler write about the German race (sometimes he called it the Aryan race)? _____
_____

14. How did Hitler and the Nazis seize power in Germany? _____
_____

15. How many civilian lives were killed because of fascism? _____
_____

16. Does fascism continue the tradition of Western political thought, begun by the Greco-Roman and Judeo-Christian cultures? How or how not? _____
_____
_____

38 Copyright © by John De Gree 2006. All rights reserved

D. Class Discussion

When you share ideas with other students, your ideas may be reinforced, rejected, or slightly changed. Listening to your classmates' ideas will help you form your own judgment.

Each student must interview at least three classmates who do not sit next to one another. The answers to the following questions must be written down on a piece of paper.

1. What is your name?
2. Compare and contrast the two totalitarian regimes of communism and fascism in terms of political philosophy, their aggressive nature, and cost in human lives.
3. How did you find your answers?

Reflection

After you have written down all your classmates' responses, think about them and ask yourself the following questions. Write down your answers under your classmates' responses.

1. What do I think of my classmates' answers?
2. Which student had the best answers to question #2 above?
3. Have I changed the way I think based on my classmates' answers?

You should now have a chance to present your ideas in a class discussion. If somebody says something with which you disagree, speak up! In your discussion, you may find out they are actually right and you are wrong. All possible viewpoints should be stated and defended out loud. Test your ideas in class.

9. World War II—Causes of Appeasement

World War II has been the largest and most tragic war of human history. Over 20.5 million civilians were murdered, 12.5 million soldiers were killed, and over 23 million soldiers were wounded. It was a war in which armies targeted whole civilian populations. The German army attempted to exterminate all Jews in the world, and it killed over 6 million, along with 5 million people Nazis deemed subhuman. Germany, Italy, Japan and the Soviet Union invaded and brutalized smaller nations, while the western, democratic countries slowly geared up for war. Consequences of this war can still be seen today in world conflicts, borders, attitudes, treaties, and many other ways.

Before World War II, the western democracies had a number of opportunities to stop or slow down the aggressors. However, throughout the 1930s, Germany, Italy, and Japan were able to get their way. In your essay, answer the question "What were the two main causes that led democratic leaders of the world to follow a policy of appeasement towards Adolf Hitler and Benito Mussolini?"

You should be familiar with these terms and people.

appeasement	the Munich Conference	Joseph Stalin
World War I	isolationism	pacifism
Axis Powers	Holocaust	Benito Mussolini
Eastern Europe	Czechoslovakia	Poland
Spanish Civil War	F.D. Roosevelt	Great Depression
Munich Conference (1938)	Winston Churchill	Allies
General Tojo		

This essay has six assignments:

Assignment	Due Date		Due Date
1. Prewriting Tasks	_____	4. Rough Draft	_____
2. Thesis Statement	_____	5. Final	_____
3. Outline	_____	6. Works Cited	_____

Prewriting Activities for Essay #9
A. Events Preceding World War II

1. The Treaty of Versailles was one of the peace treaties that ended World War I. What in the Treaty of Versailles did not seem fair to Germany? _____
_____

2. Describe Kristallnacht. Did European countries protest against Germany after Kristallnacht happened? Did the United States protest against Germany? _____
_____

3. Adolf Hitler used the Jews in Germany as a scapegoat, an excuse for all of Germany's problems. What did Hitler write about the Jews in his book *Mein Kampf?*_____
_____

4. Name two ways in which Hitler defied (went against) the Treaty of Versailles before 1937. _____
_____

5. During the Spanish Civil War, which countries sent much military support to Spain? Which side won in the war? _____
_____

6. What was the *Anschluss* (annexation) of Austria? _____
_____

7. a) What was the *Munich Conference* in 1938? _____
_____

b) What did the British prime minister announce after these talks? _____
_____

8. Who did Italy attack in 1936? What did the League of Nations do in response? _____
_____

9. The United States signed a number of neutrality acts in the 1930s. Why didn't the U.S. want to take a stand during the violence of the 1930s? _____
_____

10. a) What aggressive action did Japan commit in 1931? _____
_____

b) How did the League of Nations respond? _____
_____

c) How did Japan respond? _____

B. Appeasement as a Policy

Below are six different questions that will lead you to reasons why Great Britain and France followed a policy of appeasement towards Hitler and Mussolini. They will also help you learn why the United States and the League of Nations did nothing to challenge Japan's aggression against China.

1. How many British and French soldiers and civilians died or were wounded because of World War I? _____
_____

2. Some years after the end of World War I, many British and French felt the peace treaties that ended the war were unfair towards Germany. Describe here how the peace treaties treated Germany harshly, and perhaps unfairly. _____
_____
_____

3. What, in America's early history has led the United States to have a strong tradition of isolationism? (Hint: farewell address of George Washington) _____
_____
_____

4. From the Russian Revolution of 1917, when the communists seized power, to 1939, the world's democratic governments had a great fear of Soviet communism. The Soviet Communists, under Lenin and then Stalin, had outlawed religion, shut down all churches, killed religious leaders, murdered over 10 million innocent civilians, and ran the largest work/death camps — the Gulag — known to man. Look at a map. Why would Great Britain and France not mind a stronger Germany? _____
_____
_____

5. a) What was the Great Depression? _____
_____

b) How did the Great Depression affect the British, the French, and the Americans psychologically? (Did they feel very strong, or weak, because of their difficulties?) _____
_____

6. Pacifism: a) What is pacifism? _____
_____

b) In which countries were there many pacifists? _____
_____

C. Class Discussion

When you share ideas with other students, your ideas may be reinforced, rejected, or slightly changed. Listening to your classmates' ideas will help you form your own judgment.

Each student must interview at least three classmates who do not sit next to one another. The answers to the following questions must be written down on a piece of paper.

1. What is your name?
2. What were the two main causes that led democratic leaders of the world to follow a policy of appeasement towards Adolf Hitler and Benito Mussolini?
3. How did you find your answers?

Reflection

After you have written down all your classmates' responses, think about them and ask yourself the following questions. Write down your answers under your classmates' responses.

1. What do I think of my classmates' answers?
2. With which student do I most agree and why?
3. With which student do I most disagree and why?

You should now have a chance to present your ideas in a class discussion. If somebody says something with which you disagree, speak up! In your discussion, you may find out they are actually right and you are wrong. All possible viewpoints should be stated and defended out loud. Test your ideas in class.

10. The Cold War in Europe, 1945–1960

According to President Woodrow Wilson, the United States entered into World War I "to make the world safe for democracy." Approximately 20 years after this first Great War, the world fought an even larger and more horrific war. The U.S. goals of World War I were not completely achieved in the first conflict.

In World War II, the America perhaps had simpler goals: stop both Japan and Germany from expanding. In these two aspects, Americans achieved success. The Allies destroyed the militaristic regimes of Japan and Germany and erected new democratic societies in both of these lands. However, the peace of World War II did not bring U.S. troops home. The world still was not safe for democracy, and U.S. troops took a more active role throughout the world. After World War II, the world was split into two main camps — the Communist nations and the democratic nations. American soldiers stationed in Europe and Asia stayed and fought to counter communism and the Soviet Union. Latin America also became the battleground of ideas of communism and democracy. A new kind of war began for America and the world, the Cold War.

In your essay, trace the development of the Cold War from its beginnings through the 1950s, focusing mainly on Europe. What was the nature of the Cold War? What was at stake for the United States in the Cold War? Did one society (the Soviet Union or the United States) represent *good* and one side *bad*? What side did the United States support?

To write this essay, you should be familiar with these terms and people:

Josef Stalin	Harry Truman	Potsdam Conference
Marshall Plan	NATO	Iron Curtain
Warsaw Pact	United Nations	Nikita Kruschev
Berlin Airlift	East Berlin (1953)	communism
Poland (1953)	Hungary (1956)	A. Solzhenitsyn
racial segregation	gulag	George Kennan

This essay has six assignments:

Assignment	Due Date		Due Date
1. Prewriting Tasks	_____	4. Rough Draft	_____
2. Thesis Statement	_____	5. Final	_____
3. Outline	_____	6. Works Cited	_____

Prewriting Activities for Essay #10
A. Taking Notes

Follow the structure below to write notes.

Josef Stalin
What?
Who?
When?
Where?
What does the life of Stalin tell us about the Soviet Union?
Source:

Harry Truman
What?
Who?
When?
Where?
What does the life of Truman tell us about the United States?
Source:

Gulag
What?
Who?
When?
Where?
What do the facts of the gulag tell you about the Soviet Union and communism?
Source:

Copyright © by John De Gree 2006. All rights reserved

B. Compare and Contrast

To compare means to look at two or more objects and recognize what they have in common. To contrast means to look at two or more objects and recognize what they have different from each other.

The United States and the Soviet Bloc, 1945–1960

1. In the United States, how did somebody become the president? How many presidents did the U.S. have between 1945 and 1960? _____
_____

2. In the Soviet Union, how did somebody become the general secretary of the Communist party (this means, leader of the country)? How many general secretaries did the Soviet Union have between 1945 and 1960? _____
_____

3. In the United States, what kinds of freedom did a person have regarding his job? Could he choose his own profession? Could he start a business if he wanted to? _____
_____

4. In the Soviet Union and Eastern Europe, what kinds of freedom did a person have regarding his job? Could he choose his own profession? Could he start a business if he wanted to? _____
_____

5. Were free speech and free thought protected in the United States? Could an American speak or write freely, or might he be jailed for speaking against the government? _____
_____

6. Were free speech and free thought protected in the Soviet Union and Eastern Europe? Could a Soviet speak or write freely, or might he be jailed for speaking against the government? _____
_____

7. Did Americans have the freedom to practice their own religion? _____
_____

8. Did Soviets and Eastern Europeans have the freedom to practice their own religion? __
_____

9. In the United States or in the Soviet Union were there prisons for political prisoners? How many people are believed to have been prisoners there? _____
_____

10. In the Soviet Union and Eastern Europe, what could have been said to be the greatest injustice in society? _____
_____

11. In the United States, what could have been the greatest injustice in society? _____
_____
_____

C. The Cold War in Europe, 1945–1960

1. Who were the *Big Three* at the Yalta Conference? _____

2. Who were the *Big Three* at the Potsdam Conference? _____

3. What was decided for Germany at these two conferences? _____

4. Concerning democratic elections, what did the Big Three decide for Europe after the war? _____

5. After World War II, where in Europe were governments democratically elected? Where did democratic elections not take place? _____

6. Where in Europe were there uprisings in 1953 and 1956 that were put down by soldiers? _____

7. Why was the Berlin Wall created? _____

8. What happened to Estonia, Latvia, and Lithuania after World War II? _____

9. What does *satellite country* mean? Did any European country become a satellite of the Soviet Union? _____

10. What did Winston Churchill mean when he said that an iron curtain had descended on Europe? _____

11. Did any European country become a satellite of the United States? _____

12. What was the Truman doctrine? Was it ever used from 1945–1960? _____

13. Define the term *Cold War*? _____

14. What year (it's after 1960) did the Cold War end, and how did it end? _____

Copyright © by John De Gree 2006. All rights reserved

D. Class Discussion

When you share ideas with other students, your ideas may be reinforced, rejected, or slightly changed. Listening to your classmates' ideas will help you form your own judgment.

Each student must interview at least three classmates who do not sit next to one another. The answers to the following questions must be written down on a piece of paper.

1. What was the nature of the Cold War?
2. What was at stake for the United States in the Cold War?
3. Was there a good side and a bad side?
4. What side did the United States support?

Reflection

After you have written down all your classmates' responses, think about them and ask yourself the following questions. Write down your answers under your classmates' responses.

1. What do I think of my classmates' answers?
2. With which student do I most agree and why?
3. With which student do I most disagree and why?

You should now have a chance to present your ideas in a class discussion. If somebody says something with which you disagree, speak up! In your discussion, you may find out they are actually right and you are wrong. All possible viewpoints should be stated and defended out loud. Test your ideas in class.

11. The Cold War in Asia, Africa, and Latin America, 1945–1980

According to President Woodrow Wilson, the United States entered into World War I "to make the world safe for democracy." Approximately 20 years after this first Great War, the world fought an even larger and more horrific war. The U.S. goals of World War I were not completely achieved in the first conflict.

In World War II, the United States perhaps had simpler goals: stop both Japan and Germany from expanding. In these two aspects, Americans achieved success. The Allies destroyed the militaristic regimes of Japan and Germany and erected new democratic societies in both of these lands. However, the peace of World War II did not bring U.S. troops home. The world still was not safe for democracy, and U.S. troops took a more active role throughout the world. After World War II, the world was split into two main camps — the Communist nations and the democratic nations. American soldiers stationed in Europe and Asia stayed and fought to counter communism and the Soviet Union. Latin America also became the battleground of ideas of communism and democracy. A new kind of war began for America and the world, the Cold War.

In your essay, trace the development of the Cold War from its beginnings up to 1980, focusing mainly on Asia. What was the nature of the Cold War? What was at stake for the United States in the Cold War? Did one society (the Communist or the democratic) represent *good*, and one side *bad*? What side did the United States support?

To write this essay, you should be familiar with these terms and people:

Mao Tse-Tung	communism	Harry Truman	cultural revolution
Truman doctrine	Potsdam Conference	SEATO	the Vietnamese War
United Nations	Cuban Missile Crisis	Guatemala	Angola
the Congo Republic	the Korean War	Egypt and the Suez Canal (1956)	
Organization of American States (OAS)			

This essay has six assignments:

Assignment	Due Date		Due Date
1. Prewriting Tasks	_____	4. Rough Draft	_____
2. Thesis Statement	_____	5. Final	_____
3. Outline	_____	6. Works Cited	_____

Prewriting Activities for Essay #11
A. Taking Notes

Follow the structure below to write notes as they pertain to the Cold War, 1945–1980.

Mao Tse-Tung (Zedong)
What?
Who?
When?
Where?
What does the life of Mao tell us about China?
Source:

Harry Truman
What?
Who?
When?
Where?
What does the life of Truman tell us about the United States?
Source:

The Cultural Revolution
What?
Who?
When?
Where?
What do the facts of the Chinese Cultural Revolution tell you about China and communism?
Source:

B. Compare and Contrast

The United States, Democracy, and the Communist World, 1945–1980

1. In the United States, how did somebody become the president? How many presidents did the U.S. have between 1945 and 1980? _____
_____

2. In China, the leader used to be called the Chairman of the Communist party. How many Chairmen did China have between 1945 and 1980? _____
_____

3. In the United States, what kinds of freedom did a person have, regarding his? Could he choose his own profession? Could he start a business if he wanted to? _____
_____

4. In China and Communist countries of Asia and Latin America, what kinds of freedom did a person have, regarding his job? Could he choose his own profession? Could he start a business if he wanted to? _____
_____

5. Were free speech and free thought protected in the United States? Could an American speak or write freely, or might he be jailed for speaking against the government? _____
_____

6. Were free speech and free thought protected in Communist Asia and Africa? Could a Communist Vietnamese speak or write freely, or might he be jailed for speaking against the government? _____
_____

7. From 1945 to 1980, how many people were put to death by Communist governments? During the same time, how many people did the United States and pro–American governments put to death? _____
_____

8. Did Communist Asians, Africans, and Latin Americans have the freedom to practice their own religion? _____
_____

9. In the United States or in Communist Asia, were there prisons for political prisoners? Where in the world were there death squads? (Death squads were secret police that killed political enemies.)_____
_____

10. Which society fostered greater injustices, the Communist or the democratic? _____
_____
_____

C. The Cold War in Asia, Latin America, and Africa, 1945–1980

1. Define the term *Cold War*? _____
_____
_____

2. What was the Truman doctrine? Was it ever used from 1945 to 1980? _____
_____
_____

3. Describe the U.S. policy of *containment* towards communism. _____
_____

4. In the Middle East, of which country in the late 1940s was the United States an ally? ___

5. Which country did the Soviet Union support in the Middle East in the 1950s? _____

6. Who set up a pro-Communist government in Iraq in July 1958? _____

7. In the Republic of the Congo, which type of government was formed after independence was won from France in 1960? _____

8. In Angola in 1975, Angola won its independence from Portugal. Describe the situation that followed in Angola. _____
_____

9. Why did many Cubans support Fidel Castro in the Cuban revolution of 1959? What type of government did he set up? _____
_____

10. Very briefly describe the Cuban Missile Crisis. _____
_____

11. Describe a brief political history of Chile, from 1970 to 1980. _____
_____

12. Describe what happened in Guatemala from 1950 to 1980. _____
_____

13. What was the Korean War? _____
_____

14. What was the Vietnam War? _____
_____

D. Class Discussion

When you share ideas with other students, your ideas may be reinforced, rejected, or slightly changed. Listening to your classmates' ideas will help you form your own judgment.

Each student must interview at least three classmates who do not sit next to one another. The answers to the following questions must be written down on a piece of paper.

1. What was the nature of the Cold War in Africa, Latin America, and Asia?
2. What was at stake for the United States in the Cold War?
3. Was there a good side and a bad side?
4. What side did the United States support?

Reflection

After you have written down all your classmates' responses, think about them and ask yourself the following questions. Write down your answers under your classmates' responses.

1. What do I think of my classmates' answers?
2. With which student do I most agree and why?
3. With which student do I most disagree and why?

You should now have a chance to present your ideas in a class discussion. If somebody says something with which you disagree, speak up! In your discussion, you may find out they are actually right and you are wrong. All possible viewpoints should be stated and defended out loud. Test your ideas in class.

12. Create Your Own Assignment

You have had much practice in researching and writing persuasive essays in history. As your last research assignment of the year, create your own thesis, on a topic of your choice. Choose from a list of possible thesis topics — examples are below — or make your own.

The Development of Western Political Thought, from Ancient Greece to Today

The Cold War in Asia, 1945–1960

The Cold War in Asia, 1960–1989

The Cold War in Europe, 1960–1989

The Cold War in Latin America, 1945–1989

The Establishment of Israel

Nationalism in the Middle East

The Collapse of the Soviet Union

Mao Tse-Tung and Communist China

The End of Imperialism

The European Community

Post–Soviet Union: The Formation of New Countries

Communism versus Capitalism

Terror as a Political Tool

Religion in the Twentieth Century

Space Exploration

Technology

Cultural Movements of the Twentieth Century

Part Two: Social Studies Literacy Skills

Chapter II: Skills for a One-Paragraph Essay

1. Fact or Opinion?

Fact

A **fact** in history is a statement that is accepted as true and is not debatable. A fact often refers to a date, a person, or a document. For example, "The Declaration of Independence was written and signed in 1776." We know this happened because we have the original document, the men who wrote and signed this document wrote about it, and observers wrote about it as well. There is no doubt in anybody's mind whether the facts in this statement are true.

Which of the following sentences are facts?

Fact or Not a Fact?
1. _____The American Revolution freed all the slaves in America.
2. _____All American Indians were happy about the arrival of Europeans.
3. _____In World War II, the Soviet Union lost.
4. _____Ronald Reagan was U.S. president from 1976 to 1984.
5. _____Global warming caused the hottest day in the year 2004.

Opinion

An **opinion** is an expression of somebody's ideas and is debatable. Opinions that are based on facts and good reasoning are stronger than opinions not based on facts. In history, opinions alone tend to be less persuasive than when a person supports his opinions with facts.

Which of the following are opinions and which are facts?

Opinion or Fact?
1. _____Western political thought is harmful to people.
2. _____The French Revolution happened after the American Revolution.
3. _____The U.S. Constitution created the best government in the world.
4. _____Napoleon Bonaparte conquered almost all of Europe.
5. _____Napoleon Bonaparte was a mean and cruel leader.

Now that you've learned the difference between fact and opinion, read the example paragraphs below and answer the questions.

Student 1:   One hundred years ago, life in the United States and in the world was kinder to children and to all people. Older people didn't get upset at the youth for making too much noise or for running around barefoot. Neighbors watched out for each other and were very friendly with each other. Because there weren't any cars, the pace of life was slower and nobody rushed around all day. Women were treated with respect and dignity, and boys were taught at a young age how to be responsible. There were fewer problems a long time ago. Everybody just worked hard to make a living, helped each other out, and tried hard to get along.

Student 2:   One hundred years ago life in the United States was harder on children and on all people. In the United States, families were so poor that children had to work all day. It wasn't until the 1930s, with Franklin Delano Roosevelt's New Deal, that labor laws restricted children from working like adults. Before the 1960s, the policy of racial discrimination known as "segregation" ruled in many states. In Santa Ana, California, for example, there were separate schools for whites, for blacks, and for Hispanics. It wasn't until court orders, like *Brown v. Board of Education* (1954), and the Civil Rights Act (1964) where blacks and other minorities began to see the full rights of U.S. citizens.

Questions
1. Which of these two students uses more opinion than fact? _____

2. Copy one sentence that is an opinion. _____

3. Copy one sentence that details at least one fact. _____

4. Which of these two students' writings is more persuasive? Why? _____

2. Judgment

Judgment in social studies means a person's evaluation of facts. For example, the French Revolution began in 1789. This year was a very important one for France. The fact in these sentences is that the French Revolution began in 1789. The judgment is that this year was an important one for France. Good judgment is very persuasive but bad judgment is not. Make one judgment per each fact below. Discuss your judgments in class.

Fact:	Adolf Hitler was responsible for the murder of 11 million people in concentration camps.
Judgment:	Hitler was an evil person.
Fact:	Franklin Delano Roosevelt was elected a record four times as U.S. President.
Judgment:	Americans greatly trusted Roosevelt to be the leader of the country.

Make your own.

Fact:
Judgment:
Fact:
Judgment:
Fact:
Judgment:

3. Supporting Evidence

Supporting evidence refers to everything you use to support your thesis. These include, but are not limited to, the following:

1. Diaries and journals
2. Government documents, such as birth certificates
3. Songs and stories
4. Coins, medals, jewelry
5. Artistic works such as pictures and paintings
6. Tools and pottery
7. Documents, such as the Declaration of Independence
8. Weapons
9. Burial remains
10. Literature and customs

Good writers overwhelm the reader with so many pieces of supporting evidence that the writing will be quickly accepted. Also, the writer has a duty to explain carefully and logically the meaning of the evidence, showing how it supports the thesis. A writer must be careful, however, not to include unnecessary evidence. For example, the fact that Lincoln was born in a log cabin isn't evidence that he was a good president. Also, the dates a president was born and died may be evidence, but they would not support a thesis arguing who was the best president.

Practice
With your teacher discuss which of the following is evidence for the topic "Explain what daily life was like in Prussia in the 1700s.
1. A diary from 1984
2. A newspaper article from 1799
3. Your friend likes the subject
4. A documentary about Prussian life in the 1700s
5. A Prussian song written and sung in 1777
6. Information on Prussia's leaders of the 1800s
7. A painting of farm life in 1600s Prussia

4. Primary or Secondary Source Analysis

A **primary source** is a piece of evidence authored by a person who witnessed or experienced a historical event. For example, diaries and journals are primary sources. It is usually better to find out something from a person who experienced a particular event than to hear about it secondhand. Primary source documents are usually the most useful for historians.

A **secondary source** is a piece of evidence developed by somebody who was not a witness to the historical event. Examples of secondary sources are textbooks, documentaries, and encyclopedias. Secondary sources are valuable but not as valuable as primary sources. Secondary sources contain the bias of the writer. This means that the writer of a secondary source will put his own ideas into his explanation of the historical event, even when he may be trying not to.

> Take a look at these two examples regarding the same event, a car accident outside of school.

Example 1: "Oh no! I was in the back seat of my mom's car. This kid threw his friend's handball onto the street. All of a sudden, his friend jumped in front of my mom's car to get his ball. He didn't even look if a car was coming. My mom hit him and his body smashed against our windshield. Blood was everywhere!"

Example 2: "Did you hear what happened? Mario told me that his brother was walking home when he dropped his handball onto the street. After his brother looked both ways for cars, he stepped out onto the street to get his ball. Then this mad lady came speeding down the street and aimed her car at him. She hit him on purpose!"

Questions
1. Which is a primary source? _____
2. Which is a secondary source? _____
3. Which of these is more believable? Why? _____

Copyright © by John De Gree 2006. All rights reserved

5. Using Quotes

An effective analytical essay in social studies will use quotes. For example, an essay about the Declaration of Independence will be stronger if certain passages from this document are used. When you argue a point about the past, there is no better evidence than a quote from a primary source. Also, when you use quotes, it is essential that you frame the quote. Before the quote is used, you need to introduce it. Introducing a quote means to write the original author's name and the speech or document from which the quote was taken, and to explain the quote briefly. Then write the quote. After you write the quote, tell the reader the meaning of the quote. It is your job to lead the reader through the quote so your main point is emphasized. Do not imagine the reader will understand exactly what you mean, unless you tell the reader exactly what you are thinking.

Look at the example below. The paragraph is part of an answer to the question "According to Thomas Jefferson, is there anybody in society who should have more rights than others?"

According to Thomas Jefferson, all men should have the same rights in society. In the Declaration of Independence, Jefferson writes, "All men are created equal; they are endowed by their Creator with certain unalienable rights; that among these are life, liberty, and the pursuit of happiness." This means that each person should be treated equally under the law. Whether you are rich or poor, or whether your family is famous or not, all citizens should have the same rights.

Practice
Practice writing three quotations taken from your textbook. Use correct punctuation.

1. _____
_____
_____
_____

2. _____
_____
_____
_____

3. _____
_____
_____
_____

6. Paraphrasing

Paraphrasing means to take information from your research and to put it in your own words. This is an important skill to have when writing a research paper. If you copy directly from a source such as a book, but do not place the words in quotation marks and write the author's name, it is called **plagiarism**. Plagiarism is against the rules of writing and your teacher will not accept the work! The law may punish a professor or an author for plagiarizing.

Here is an example of paraphrasing a quote from a teacher.

Quote: "In 1914, European nations began a war that was caused by dislike and hatred among countries. The United States tried to stay out of the war by being neutral. After German sailors aboard a submarine killed Americans on the British ship the *Lusitania*, President Woodrow Wilson grew to believe that Germany was a danger, and he persuaded the U.S. Congress to declare war in 1917."

Paraphrase: European nations began fighting World War I because of old rivalries. Woodrow Wilson's attempt to keep the United States out of the war succeeded for some time. Nevertheless, German actions affected American citizens. A German submarine destroyed the British ship, the *Lusitania*. Americans were on this ship and dies. The United States declared war in 1917.

Practice
Quote: "Although Joseph Stalin and the Soviet Communists are responsible for the killing of over 20 million of their own people, Hitler and the Nazis are better known for their murderous ways."
Paraphrase: _____
_____
_____
_____

Quote: "The French military officer Napoleon Bonaparte knew how to handle a riotous mob. To quell a protest, he ordered his soldiers to fire a cannon directly into civilians. Instead of firing a cannonball, however, Bonaparte ordered his soldiers to pack scrap metal, nails, and bullets into the cannon. This way, more protesters would be killed or wounded."
Paraphrase: _____
_____
_____
_____
_____

7. Thesis Statement

The **thesis statement** is the main idea or argument of your entire essay. It is your judgment regarding the essay question and it should contain words used in the prompt. A thesis statement is not a fact. Instead, it is your judgment of the facts. Because of this, a thesis has to be something with which not everyone will agree. Every thesis will provide an answer to the prompt and a few reasons of support.

Here is an example from essay question #1 in this book: "Defend or reject the statement 'Western political thought and the societies from which it originated are based on ideas that are detrimental to humanity.'

Example 1: Western political thought and the societies from which it originated are detrimental to humanity because the weak are not given extra help, the strong are allowed to rule the weak, and the rich are allowed to abuse the poor.

This thesis answers the question and provides an outline for the rest of the essay. The reader addresses the question directly and provides general reasons to support his answer. In the essay, the writer will expand on these reasons.

Come up with two more examples of a thesis based on this first question.

Example 2: _____

Example 3: _____

The Good Thesis Test

If you can answer, "Yes," to these questions, you most likely have a good thesis for a one-paragraph essay:

1. Does the thesis address the prompt directly?
2. Does the thesis take a position that I can argue with evidence?
3. Could somebody argue against my thesis statement?

8. Conclusion

The **conclusion** ties the evidence presented in the essay back to the thesis statement. It is the writer's last chance to present how the evidence supports the thesis statement. In a one-paragraph essay the conclusion can be one sentence, but it may be more.

Here is an example answering the question "Why did the Communists have success in Russia?" The last sentence in this paragraph is the conclusion.

Communism had success in Russia in large part because of World War I. During World War I, Russia experienced great losses at the hands of the German and Austro-Hungarian armies. Over 1.7 million Russian soldiers were killed and nearly 5 million were wounded in World War I. German soldiers occupied parts of Russia. Many Russian soldiers went into battle without guns and would scavenge among the dead soldiers to find a weapon. Vladimir Lenin, leader of the Russian Bolshevik (later called Communist) party, pushed for an end to the unpopular war. One of the first acts of the Bolshevik party was to admit defeat to the Germans and drop out of World War I by signing the Treaty of Brest-Litovsk in 1918. **Partly because of Russia's failures in World War I, Russians turned to the Communists for leadership.**

The Good Conclusion Test

If you can answer, "Yes," to these questions, you have written a good conclusion:

1. Does the conclusion restate the thesis?
2. Does the conclusion include the pieces of evidence from my essay?
3. Does the conclusion help convince the reader that the thesis is correct?

9. Outline for a One-Paragraph Essay

An **outline** helps you organize your thoughts and shows if you have enough evidence to support your thesis statement. An outline does not need to be written in complete sentences, except for the thesis statement and the conclusion. The more evidence you include, the stronger your argument will be.

An example outline follows to the essay question "Why did the Communists have success in Russia?"

I. Thesis Statement: Communism had success in Russia in large part because of World War I.

II. Supporting Evidence:
1. Russia was losing World War I
2. 1.7 million dead, nearly 5 million wounded
3. German occupation
4. No guns
5. Lenin was anti-war
6. Brest-Litovsk Peace Treaty, 1918

III. Conclusion: Partly because of Russia's failures in World War I, Russians turned to the Communists for leadership.

Following this page are two forms, a "Basic Outline Form for a One-Paragraph Essay" and an "Advanced Outline Form for a One-Paragraph Essay." Your teacher will determine which form you will use. The basic outline is for the beginning historian and the advanced outline is for the more developed and motivated historian. Which one are you?

Basic Outline Form for a One-Paragraph Essay
(Use complete sentences for the thesis statement and the conclusion.)

I. Thesis Statement: _____

_____

    A.   Supporting Evidence_____

    B.   Supporting Evidence_____

    C.   Supporting Evidence_____

II. Conclusion: _____

Advanced Outline Form for a One-Paragraph Essay
(Use complete sentences for the thesis statement and the conclusion.)

I. Thesis Statement: _____

_____

    A. Supporting Evidence_____

    B. Supporting Evidence_____

    C. Supporting Evidence _____

    D. Supporting Evidence _____

    E. Supporting Evidence_____

II. Conclusion: _____

Copyright © by John De Gree 2006. All rights reserved

10. Rough Draft for a One-Paragraph Essay

The **rough draft** is the first time that you will explain all the supporting evidence that you use. To do this, take your outline and explain how your evidence supports the thesis statement. Instead of listing your evidence, you will explain its importance. Here is an example of a rough draft of a paragraph based on the question "Why did the Communists have success in Russia?" (The sentences in bold are those that explain how your evidence supports the thesis.)

> Communism had success in Russia in large part because of World War I. **In 1917, Russia was clearly losing World War I.** German and Austro-Hungarian troops occupied Russia 300 miles east of its former border. After 1915, Russian soldiers reportedly went into battle without weapons, hoping to pick up rifles from fallen fighters. By the end off 1917, over 1.7 million Russians had been killed, and nearly 5 million more were wounded. The war cost led to starvation and poverty among civilians. **This great tragedy for Russia opened the way for anti-government forces. Because the Czar Nicholas II continued the war effort and did not successfully address starvation and poverty, he became extremely unpopular. Many Russians turned to anti-war leaders for answers.** Vladimir Lenin was one of these leaders. He promised that once in power he would end the war immediately with Germany. After seizing power through a revolution, Lenin took Russia out of the war with the Brest-Litovsk Treaty of 1918. Even though this treaty meant that Russia lost land to Germany and the Austro-Hungarian Empire, **Russians supported it and the Communist decision to end the war because of the poor conditions of the Russian population.** In conclusion, partly because of Russia's failures in World War I, the Communists were able to seize power.

On this page and the next are the basic and advanced rough draft forms for a one-paragraph essay.

Basic Rough Draft Form for a One-Paragraph Essay
(Use complete sentences.)

I. **Thesis Statement**: _____
_____

A. Supporting Evidence: First of all, _____
_____

Explanation: (Explain how the evidence supports the topic sentence) _____
_____

B. Supporting Evidence: Secondly, _____
_____

Explanation: (Explain how the evidence supports the topic sentence) _____
_____

II. **Conclusion**: In conclusion, _____
_____

Advanced Rough Draft Form for a One-Paragraph Essay
(Use complete sentences.)

I. **Thesis Statement**: _____
_____

    A. Supporting Evidence: First of all, _____
_____

Explanation (Explain how this supports the topic sentence): _____
_____

    B. Supporting Evidence: Secondly, _____
_____

Explanation (Explain how this supports the topic sentence): _____
_____

    C. Supporting Evidence: Thirdly, _____
_____

Explanation (Explain how this supports the topic sentence): _____
_____

    D. Supporting Evidence: In addition, _____
_____

Explanation (Explain how this supports the topic sentence): _____
_____

    E. Supporting Evidence: Furthermore, _____
_____

Explanation (Explain how this supports the topic sentence): _____
_____

II. **Conclusion**: _____
_____

Chapter III: Skills for a Five-Paragraph Essay

11. Taking Notes

All research papers require the student to read, analyze, and write information that is helpful in answering the question asked. The structure of your note taking depends on the question. Before reading, structure your notes in a way so you will focus on important information and not on unimportant details that would take valuable time. Below is an example of a structure of notes based on the question "What was the key factor in destroying the idea of the divine right of kings?" Notice that the last question helps you stick to your topic.

Nationalism
What?
Who?
When?
Where?
Why?
Did this play a role in destroying the idea of the divine right of kings?
Source and page(s):

When taking notes be sure to list the source. You can do this quickly by writing only the last name of the author and the page on which you found the information. This will save you much time later when you are documenting the source in your essay. When you are writing your final essay you don't want to be stuck in the position of rummaging through your papers or flipping through your book, trying to find exactly from where you took your information. You also don't want to lie about your source. It is wrong, and your teacher may be smarter than you realize. Make sure to list your source!

12. Thesis Statement for a Five-Paragraph Essay

The **thesis statement** is the main idea or argument of your entire essay. It is your judgment regarding the essay question and it should contain words used in the prompt. A thesis statement is not a fact. Instead, it is your judgment of the evidence. Because of this, a thesis has to be something with which not everyone will agree. Every thesis will provide an answer to the prompt and a few reasons of support. In a five-paragraph essay, you should list three pieces of evidence in your thesis in order to provide the reader with an outline of your essay.

Here is an example from essay question #4 in this book, "In what field did inventions or discoveries cause the greatest change in the everyday life of humans?" Because this essay requires a five-paragraph response, the student will need three supporting pieces of evidence for the main body. These three should be included in the thesis.

Example 1: Discoveries in medicine caused the greatest change in the everyday life of humans because they increased the standard of living, helped the average person live longer, and increased the population.

This thesis answers the question and provides an outline for paragraphs two, three, and four. Paragraph two will detail how advances in medicine increased the standard of living, paragraph three how medicine changed life expectancies, and paragraph four how medicine increased the population. Come up with two more examples for a five-paragraph essay based on this question.

Example 2: _____
Example 3: _____

The Good Thesis Test
If you can answer, "Yes," to these questions, you most likely have a good thesis for a five-paragraph essay:

1. Does my thesis address the prompt directly?
2. Does my thesis take a position that I can argue with evidence?
3. Could somebody argue against my thesis statement?

13. The Topic Sentence and the Closer

The **topic sentence** is the main idea of a paragraph in the body of a multiple-paragraph essay. In a five-paragraph essay, a topic sentence takes one of the pieces of evidence in the thesis and states it strongly. The body of this paragraph will support the topic sentence.

Here is one example of a topic sentence for the question of essay #4, "In what field did inventions or discoveries cause the greatest change in the everyday life of humans?"

Thesis Statement: Discoveries in medicine caused the greatest change in the everyday life of humans because they increased the quality of life, helped the average person live longer, and increased the population.

Topic Sentence for Paragraph Two: Discoveries in medicine caused the greatest change in the everyday life of humans because they increased the quality of life.

Write a topic sentence for paragraph three in the box below.

Paragraph Three: _____

The Closer

The **closer** ties the evidence presented in the paragraph back to the topic sentence. It is the writer's last chance to present how the evidence supports the topic sentence before moving on.

Here is an example regarding the same essay question as above. The last sentence in this essay is the closer. It shows how the two details of this paragraph support the topic sentence.

Discoveries in medicine caused the greatest change in the everyday life of humans because they increased the quality of life. When people hear the term *standard of living*, they often think of how much money a person makes, what kind of a house they live in, or what kind of a car they drive. However, standard of living also refers to the quality of life a person has. In the 1800s and 1900s, medicine provided for people a higher quality of life. Edward Jenner created a vaccine to prevent smallpox. Before this vaccination, smallpox claimed lives of many or left scars on those who survived. Louis Pasteur continued this work by creating vaccines that treated humans and animals for rabies and anthrax. **The discoveries of Edward Jenner and Louis Pasteur in medicine increased the quality of life for the average person.**

14. Outlining a Five-Paragraph Essay

An **outline** is a skeleton for your essay. Here, you organize your essay before writing it out in complete sentences. If you have a framework first, it will be fairly easy to write the essay. Below is an explanation of writing an outline for a five-paragraph essay.

   A. First Paragraph: For the first paragraph, write down the thesis and list the three topics that will be your body paragraphs.

   B. Body Paragraphs
      1. Organize your paragraphs into topics by following the order you wrote in the thesis. Your thesis should have listed three topics. The first will be the topic of your second paragraph, the second the topic of your third, and the third the topic of your fourth paragraph.

      2. You do not need to write complete sentences for your outline. It is enough to write the topics of each paragraph and to list the supporting evidence for your topic sentence in your outline. You will add more information when you write your draft.

      3. Document each source! Write the author's last name and the page where you found this information.

   C. Conclusion
   The conclusion is the place where you restate your thesis and your topic sentences. You will convince the reader better by a reminder at the end what your essay was all about. After the restatements, finish the essay with strong words supporting your thesis.

Following this page are two forms—one basic and one advanced—to help you develop your outline.

Basic Outline Form for a Five-Paragraph Essay
(Use complete sentences for the thesis, topic sentences, closers, and conclusion.)

Paragraph I.
Thesis Statement:_____
_____

Paragraph II.
I. Topic Sentence: _____
_____
     A. Supporting Evidence:_____
     B. Supporting Evidence:_____
II. Closer: _____
_____Write the source:_____

Paragraph III.
I. Topic Sentence: _____
_____
     A. Supporting Evidence:_____
     B. Supporting Evidence:_____
II. Closer: _____
_____Write the source:_____

Paragraph IV.
I. Topic Sentence: _____
_____
     A. Supporting Evidence:_____
     B. Supporting Evidence:_____
II. Closer: _____
_____Write the source:_____

Paragraph V. Conclusion
I. Restate thesis statement: _____
_____
II. Strong statement that shows how the topic sentences support the thesis:_____
_____

Advanced Outline Form for a Five-Paragraph Essay
(Use complete sentences for the thesis, topic sentences, closers, and conclusion.)

Paragraph I.
Thesis Statement: _____
_____

Paragraph II.
I. Topic Sentence: _____
_____
      A. Supporting Evidence:_____
      B. Supporting Evidence: _____
      C. Supporting Evidence:_____
      D. Supporting Evidence:_____
      E. Supporting Evidence:_____
II. Closer: _____
_____Write the source:_____

Paragraph III.
I. Topic Sentence: _____
_____
      A. Supporting Evidence:_____
      B. Supporting Evidence: _____
      C. Supporting Evidence:_____
      D. Supporting Evidence:_____
      E. Supporting Evidence:_____
II. Closer: _____
_____Write the source:_____

Paragraph IV. Use another page or the back of this paper.

Paragraph V. Conclusion
I. Restate thesis statement: _____
_____

II. Strong statement that shows how the topic sentences support the thesis:_____
_____
_____

Copyright © by John De Gree 2006. All rights reserved

15. Writing a Rough Draft for a Five-Paragraph Essay

A.   Introductory Paragraph
The social studies essay begins directly with the thesis. Following the thesis is a brief explanation of the main topics that will be written in detail in the body paragraphs. Below is an example from the essay question "Why did the Communists have success in Russia?"

The Communists had success in Russia because of the Russian failures in World War I, the bold leadership and dynamic personality of Vladimir Lenin, and the transformation of Russian society from a medieval peasant culture to a modern, technological state. In 1917, Russia faced a number of very difficult challenges. The Central Powers (Germany, Austro-Hungarian empire, the Ottoman empire) were clearly winning the war. Disaffection with the war caused many Russians to turn to anti-war leaders. Lenin was anti-war, but he was seen as a dynamic and forceful leader. Lastly, Russian society resembled the medieval world of serf and master, and it was in the midst of great social upheaval. These three reasons led Russia to the arms of the Communists, who promised radical changes.

B.   The Body
The body of your essay is where you present your evidence to prove your thesis. In these paragraphs, you will present your evidence and explain how it supports the topic sentence. An example of this is found in Skill #10, Rough Draft for a One-Paragraph Essay. Keep the order of your arguments the same as the order of mention in the thesis. Attempt to order the events chronologically.

C.   Conclusion
In this paragraph, you need to restate your thesis, tie the topic sentences of your body paragraphs to the thesis, and leave the reader with the strongest evidence that supports your argument. Your job is to convince the reader that your position is correct. Write strongly!

Following this page are two forms—one basic and one advanced—to help you develop your rough draft.

Basic Rough Draft Form for a Five-Paragraph Essay
(Use complete sentences. Use the back when you need space.)

Paragraph I.
Thesis Statement: _____
_____

Paragraph II.
Topic Sentence: _____
_____

A. Supporting Evidence: First of all, _____
_____

Explanation (Explain how the evidence supports the thesis): _____
_____

B. Supporting Evidence: Secondly, _____
_____

Explanation (Explain how the evidence supports the thesis): _____
_____

II. Closer: In conclusion, _____
_____

Paragraphs III and IV. Follow the structure of Paragraph II.

Paragraph V. Conclusion
I. Restate thesis statement: _____
_____

II. Strong statement that shows how the topic sentences support the thesis: ____
_____

Advanced Rough Draft Form for a Five-Paragraph Essay
(Use complete sentences.)

Paragraph I.
Thesis Statement: _____
_____

Paragraph II.
I. Topic Sentence: _____
_____

A. Supporting Evidence: First of all, _____
_____

Explanation (Explain how this supports the thesis): _____
_____

B. Supporting Evidence: Secondly, _____
_____

Explanation (Explain how this supports the thesis): _____
_____

C. Supporting Evidence: Thirdly, _____
_____

Explanation (Explain how this supports the thesis): _____
_____

D. Supporting Evidence: In addition, _____
_____

Explanation (Explain how this supports the thesis): _____
_____

E. Supporting Evidence: Furthermore, _____
_____

Explanation (Explain how this supports the thesis): _____
_____

II. Closer: _____
_____

Paragraphs III and IV. Follow the same structure as above.

Paragraph V. Conclusion
I. Restate thesis statement: _____
_____

II. Strong statement that shows how the topic sentences support the thesis:
_____
_____

16. Revising

After writing the rough draft, it is necessary to revise. Revising involves four steps. Take your essay and perform these four tasks with a red pen in hand.

STEP I Deletion

Delete dead words: the end, every, just, nice, great, bad, got, everything, getting, so, well, a lot, lots, get, good, some, yours, you, your, very

STEP II Addition

A. Add words, facts, or better descriptions. Imagine you are writing for an adult who does not know the subject well. Explain every point precisely.
B. Use transitions whenever helpful.

To add ideas
further, furthermore, moreover, in addition

To show results
therefore, consequently, as a result

To indicate order
first, second, in addition to

To summarize
to sum up, to summarize, in short

To compare
similarly, likewise, by comparison

Conclusion
in conclusion, to conclude, finally

STEP III Substitution

Substitute repetitive or weak words.
A. Underline the first word in each sentence. If the words are the same, change some of the words.
B. Read your thesis, topic sentences, closers, and conclusion; change words as needed. Is your word choice powerful and effective? Will your essay convince the reader?

STEP IV Rearrangement

Write sentences that have a variety of beginnings.

Adjective beginnings
Well-equipped, dedicated Union soldiers won the American Civil War.

"ing" words
Riding horses was common among most 1800s Americans.

Prepositional phrases
Over the vast Pacific Ocean, Columbus sailed.

Dependent clause
Because of Lincoln, the North did not give up the war effort.

"ly" words
Bravely, Washington led the Continental Army to victory.

Adverbs
Slowly, but surely, Grant moved the Union Army

17. Documenting Sources in the Text

When you take information from a source and use it in a paragraph, you cite it at the end of the paragraph. Place in parentheses the author's name and the page number on which you found the information. For example, if you've found information on the Russian Revolution from a book written by Robert De Gree you would document it as in the example below.

> Communism had success in Russia in large part because of World War I. In 1917, Russia was clearly losing World War I. German and Austro-Hungarian troops occupied Russia 300 miles east of its former border. After 1915, Russian soldiers reportedly went into battle without weapons, hoping to pick up rifles from fallen fighters. By the end of 1917, over 1.7 million Russians had been killed and nearly 5 million more were wounded. The war cost led to starvation and poverty among civilians. This great tragedy for Russia opened the way for anti-government forces. Because Czar Nicholas II continued the war effort and did not successfully address starvation and poverty, he became extremely unpopular. Many Russians turned to anti-war leaders for answers. Vladimir Lenin was one of these leaders. He promised that once in power he would end the war immediately with Germany. After seizing power through a revolution, Lenin took Russia out of the war with the Brest-Litovsk Treaty of 1918. Even though this treaty meant that Russia lost land to Germany and the Austro-Hungarian Empire, Russians supported it and the Communist decision to end the war because of the poor conditions of the Russian population. In conclusion, partly because of Russia's failures in World War I, the Communists were able to seize power. (De Gree 294).

Note: This is according to Gibaldi, Joseph, <u>MLA Handbook for Writers of Research Papers,</u> (New York: The Modern Language Association of America, 1995).

18. Works Cited

At the end of your document, on a separate piece of paper, write "Works Cited" at the top middle. After this, write your sources in alphabetical order using the following format:

Book
Author (Last Name, First Name). <u>Title of Book</u>. Place of publication: Publisher, date. (If there is more than one author, list them in alphabetical order with a comma in between names.)

Author of one chapter in a book
Author (Last Name, First Name). "Title of chapter." <u>Title of Book</u>. Place of Publication: Publisher, date. Pages of chapter.

Dictionary
<u>Title of Dictionary</u>. Edition.

Internet
Author (if known). "Document Title." <u>Website or Database Title</u>. Date of electronic publication (if known). Name of sponsoring institution (if known). Date information was accessed <URL>.

Encyclopedia
"Article." <u>Encyclopedia Title</u>. Edition.

Interview or Lecture
Name of Speaker (Last Name, First Name). "Title of interview or lecture." Place of interview or lecture, date.

Note: This is according to Gibaldi, Joseph, <u>MLA Handbook for Writers of Research Papers</u>, (New York: The Modern Language Association of America, 1995).

19. Typing Guidelines

1. All final research papers must be typed. The Works Cited page must also be typed.
2. The font must be a standard typeface and style. Courier, Helvetica, and Times are good choices. Do not use italics, handwriting, or anything else decorative.
3. The size of the letters must be 12 points.
4. All margins must be one inch from the top, bottom, and each side.
5. All sentences will be double-spaced.
6. Pages will be numbered in the lower right-hand side of the page. Do not number your Cover page. The Works Cited page is numbered but does not count as a text page.

20. The Cover Page and Checklist

Cover Page

The Cover page needs to have the title of your research paper centered. It can be at the top, the middle, or the bottom of the page. You need to make an illustration by drawing in pencil, coloring in colored pencils, or using any other teacher-approved medium.

In the bottom right-hand corner, write or type your name, date, and period of your social studies teacher.

Checklist

All final papers must have these items turned in to your social studies teacher on the final due date.

Inside of a clear, plastic folder include the following items in this order:

1. Cover page   _____
2. Final draft   _____
3. Works Cited page _____
4. Prewriting   _____
5. Outline   _____
6. Rough draft   _____

Chapter IV: Skills for a Multi-Page Essay

21. Thesis Statement for a Multi-Page Essay

As explained earlier in this book, the **thesis statement** is the main idea or argument of your entire essay. It is your judgment regarding the essay question and may contain the same words from the prompt. A thesis statement is not a fact. Instead, it is your judgment of the evidence. Because of this, a thesis has to be something with which not everyone will agree. In a multi-page essay, the writer need not list all the evidence he will present to support the thesis statement. However, general topics of evidence need to be presented so that the reader is aware of what the essay will entail.

Here is an example from the essay question "How did the Communists gain success in Russia?"

Example 1: Ivan nervously looked over his shoulder. Rows and rows of ill-clad troops, with sunken faces from starvation, trudged grudgingly behind him. He peered forward. Smoke filled the air from the bombardment. Rifles cracked right and left, and at times the deafening roar of an explosion was heard as earth and bodies were shot into the air. "What am I doing here?" Ivan thought. "I don't even have a rifle, and my boots are worn through. I hate my officer. Oh, God. Please end this war." In 1917, Ivan was a typical soldier in the Russian army. Tired, hungry, ill-clad troops, the Russian soldiers looked for someone to rescue them. The Communists promised the Russians an early end to the war, if power could be seized from Czar Nicholas II. The Communists had great success in Russia in 1918 in overthrowing the government of Russia. **Although there were many reasons for the Communists' success in violently taking control of Russia, one reason for the success of the Communist Revolution in Russia was the promise to end World War I.**

The Good Thesis Test
If you can answer, "Yes," to these questions, you most likely have a good thesis for a multi-page essay.

1. Does the thesis directly address the prompt?
2. Does my thesis take a position that I can argue with evidence?
3. Could somebody argue against my thesis statement?

22. Counterargument

In social studies, many historians have different judgments based on the same evidence. For example, some historians view the Russian Revolution and the leadership of the Communists in Russia as a great tragedy, while others feel it was a success. These are two very different judgments on world history. These two judgments can be called two perspectives. A **perspective** is a particular way of looking at an historical event.

When you defend your thesis statement, you should include at least one counterargument. A **counterargument** is an argument in which the writer presents an idea that goes against his own thesis statement. Then, in that paragraph, the writer shows how this idea is wrong.

For example, imagine if the thesis statement to an essay were, "Communism in Russia was a positive force for Russian society." The counterargument paragraph for this thesis should be at the end of the essay, perhaps right before the conclusion paragraph.

Here is an example of a counterargument paragraph:

> Some historians may claim that Communism in Russia was a negative force in Russian society. These historians are completely wrong. These historians like to point out that Communists killed somewhere between 20–40 million Soviets. Or, these historians refer to the reign of terror inflicted on society by Stalin that made neighbor report on neighbor, co-worker on co-worker. These historians, however, are missing the point. When the Communists took over in Russia, Russians had one of the world's lowest standards of living. Russian society was completely backward. Of course, a backwards society would experience hard times, when trying modernize quickly. The Communists brought Russia to the modern age in incredible speed. In a short period of twenty years (1920–1940) Russia became an industrial state, something it took the U.S. 100 years to do. Also, Russian industrialization made it strong enough to defeat Adolf Hitler and the Germans. Communism in Russia saved the West from Hitler and modernized Russian society.

Notice that the beginning of the paragraph above begins with the words "Some historians say." This is because you are presenting an idea that is opposite of yours. In your paragraph, be clear that you think these people are wrong.

23. Analyzing Primary Sources

When you read history and try to analyze it, pay attention to details of the document that tell you important details of the source. These small details can give you incredible insight as to how you should analyze the historical information. Here are a few basic questions to which you should find answers, while you are analyzing historical texts.

1. Who wrote it? What position does the writer have? Is the writer a professor, an author of novels? Is the author respected in the field? Did multiple authors prepare the text?

2. Who is the audience? Students? Bookstore customers? Newspaper readers? Magazine readers?

3. When was the text written? Was it written during a critical time of history that the text is about? Was it written many years after the time of history it is written about? Are historians more biased about events that happen during our lifetime?

4. Who paid for the text to be written? Is there a chance that the author(s) will be biased because of who is paying for the text?

5. Where was the text written? Was the text written in a place that is in the middle of the historical study the text is about? Is it possible the author can be biased based on where it was written? What country is the author from? Is it possible the country might affect someone's perspective?

6. Who is the publisher? Could the publisher have a bias that might affect the veracity (truth) of the materials?

7. Why was the text written? What was the purpose of the text? Was it meant to be part of a textbook? Was it meant to stir anti governmental, or pro governmental feelings?

Copyright © by John De Gree 2006. All rights reserved

24. Cause and Effect

Cause and effect is a term that means one event made another event happen. For example, if you push against the pedals of your bicycle, the bicycle moves. In this example, the push against the pedals is the cause and the bicycle moving is the effect.

CAUSE -------------------------------→EFFECT
push against pedals---------------→bicycle moves

In social studies, cause and effect usually relates events and people. The relationship is trickier to understand than the above example with the bicycle. Sometimes it is difficult to see causes and effects in history. Here are two examples from American history with which most historians would agree.

CAUSE ----------------------------------→EFFECT
Japan attacks Pearl Harbor---------→the United States enters World War II
the U.S. drops atomic bombs on Japan -------→Japan surrenders

Write down five examples of cause and effect based on everyday examples. The first one is done for you.

Cause	Effect
1. Jack ate 10 giant spicy burritos.	1. Jack had a stomachache.
2. _____	2. _____
3. _____	3. _____
4. _____	4. _____
5. _____	5. _____

25. Compare and Contrast

To **compare** means to look at two or more objects and recognize what they have in common. To **contrast** means to look at two or more objects and recognize what they have different from each other.

Try to compare and contrast President Reagan with President Carter.

Ronald Reagan		**Jimmy Carter**
Differences	**Similarities**	**Differences**
Republican	Both politicians	Democrat

26. Outline and Rough Draft for a Multi-Page Essay

In a longer essay, the only item that differs structurally from the smaller essays is the introductory paragraph. In smaller essays that are from one to two pages, the introduction should begin with the thesis statement. In longer essays, the writer can begin with information that will catch the reader's attention and add the thesis at the end of the paragraph. Read the sample introductory paragraph below for the essay question "Was the Civil War necessary?" Notice that the last sentence is the thesis statement.

>The American Civil War is the bloodiest war in our country's history. More than 500,000 Americans died. Brother fought against brother. Townspeople took up arms against each other. Great suffering became commonplace. Even so, because of the Civil War our nation has never faced another challenge to its unity. In over 140 years not one state has ever tried to secede or rebel from the United States. More importantly, the Civil War ended slavery on American soil. Millions of slaves were forever released from bondage into freedom. Without the Civil War, nobody knows for how long slavery would have continued. Even though the American Civil War was a tragic war; it was good and necessary.

For further help on outlining and writing a rough draft for a multi-page essay see the following pages.

Basic Outline Form for a Multi-Page Essay

(Use complete sentences for the thesis, topic sentences, closers, and conclusion.)

Paragraph I.
Thesis Statement: _____
_____

Paragraph II.
I. Topic Sentence: _____
_____
      A. Supporting Evidence:_____
      B. Supporting Evidence:_____
II. Closer: _____
_____Write the source:_____

Remaining Body Paragraphs.
Follow the same structure as paragraph II.

Paragraph V. Conclusion
I. Restate thesis statement: _____
_____

II. Strong statement that shows how the topic sentences support the thesis:
_____
_____

Advanced Outline Form for a Multi-Page Essay
(Use complete sentences for the thesis, topic sentences, closers, and conclusion.)

Paragraph I.
Thesis Statement: _____
_____

Paragraph II.
I. Topic Sentence: _____
_____
      A. Supporting Evidence: _____
      B. Supporting Evidence: _____
      C. Supporting Evidence: _____
      D. Supporting Evidence: _____
      E. Supporting Evidence: _____
II. Closer: _____
_____ Write the source: _____

Remaining Body Paragraphs.
Follow the same structure as Paragraph II.

Paragraph V. Conclusion
I. Restate thesis statement: _____
_____

II. Strong statement that shows how the topic sentences support the thesis: _____
_____

Basic Rough Draft Form for a Multi-Page Essay
(Use complete sentences. Use the back when you need space.)

Paragraph I.
Thesis Statement: _____
_____

Paragraph II.
I. Topic Sentence: _____
_____

    A. Supporting Evidence: First of all, _____
_____

Explanation (Explain how this supports the topic sentence): _____
_____

    B. Supporting Evidence: Secondly, _____
_____

Explanation (Explain how this supports the topic sentence): _____
_____

II. Closer (Show how A and B support the topic sentence): In conclusion, _____
_____

Write the source: _____

Remaining Body Paragraphs.
Follow the same structure as Paragraph II.

Paragraph V. Conclusion
I. Restate thesis statement: _____
_____

II. Strong statement that shows how the topic sentences support the thesis: ____
_____

Advanced Rough Draft Form for a Multi-Page Essay
(Use complete sentences. Use the back when you need space.)

Paragraph I.
Thesis Statement: _____
_____

Paragraph II.
I. Topic Sentence: _____
_____

    A. Supporting Evidence: _____

Explanation (Explain how this supports the topic sentence): _____
_____

    B. Supporting Evidence: _____

Explanation (Explain how this supports the topic sentence): _____
_____

    C. Supporting Evidence: _____

Explanation (Explain how this supports the topic sentence): _____
_____

    D. Supporting Evidence: _____

Explanation (Explain how this supports the topic sentence): _____
_____

    E. Supporting Evidence: _____

Explanation (Explain how this supports the topic sentence): _____
_____

II. Closer (Show how A and B support the topic sentence): _____
_____

Write the source: _____

Remaining Body Paragraphs.
Follow the same structure as Paragraph II.

Paragraph V. Conclusion
I. Restate thesis statement: _____
_____

II. Strong statement that shows how the topic sentences support the thesis: _____
_____

Chapter V: Grading Rubrics

One-Paragraph Essay Grading Rubric

Grading Scale
4   Exceeds Standards
3   Meets Standards
2   Approaching Standards
1   Below Standards
0   Nonexistent

                                                                                                                 Yes/No

I.   Thesis Statement:
      Does it persuasively answer the question?   _____
                                            Score _____

II.   Evidence Used:
      Are two or more relevant pieces of evidence used?   _____
                                            Score _____

III.   Evidence Explained
      Is the evidence explained correctly and persuasively?   _____
                                            Score _____

IV.   Conclusion:
      Does the evidence strengthen the topic sentence?   _____
                                            Score _____

V.   Prewriting Activities
      Are all prewriting activities included and attached
      to the final?   _____
                                            Score _____

                 Total Addition of Scores =   _____
                                                      <u>X 5</u>
                             Score =   _____
Spelling or Grammatical Errors   -_____
Missing Prewriting Work   -_____

                           Final Score =   _____

Five-Paragraph Essay Grading Rubric

Grading Scale
4   Exceeds Standards
3   Meets Standards
2   Approaching Standards
1   Below Standards
0   Nonexistent

Paragraph I.   Yes/No
A. Thesis: Does it answer the question and provide organizational structure? _____
B. Interest?   Does it grab the interest of the reader?   _____
                                             Score: _____

Paragraph II.
A. Topic Sentence: Does it provide a strong statement supporting the thesis? _____
B. Evidence: 1. Is evidence used to support the topic sentence? _____
                      2. Is the evidence explained clearly and in detail? _____
C. Closer: Does the closer convincingly link the evidence
                    with the topic sentence?   _____
                                               Score: _____

Paragraph III.
A. Topic Sentence: Does it provide a strong statement supporting the thesis? _____
B. Evidence: 1. Is evidence used to support the topic sentence? _____
                      2. Is the evidence explained clearly and in detail? _____
C. Closer: Does the closer convincingly link the evidence
                    with the topic sentence?
                                               _____
                                               Score: _____

Paragraph IV.
A. Topic Sentence: Does it provide a strong statement supporting the thesis? _____
B. Evidence: 1. Is evidence used to support the topic sentence? _____
                      2. Is the evidence explained clearly and in detail? _____
C. Closer: Does the closer convincingly link the evidence
                    with the topic sentence?
                                               _____
                                               Score: _____

Paragraph V.
A. Restating Topic Sentences: Are topic sentences in II, III, and IV restated? _____
B. Closer: Does the Closer persuasively show that the main ideas of
    paragraphs II, III, and IV strongly support the thesis?   _____

                                               Score: _____ X 5 = _____
                               Spelling or Grammatical Errors   - _____
                               Missing Prewriting Work   - _____

                               Total Score   _____

Multi-Page Essay Grading Rubric

Grading Scale
4   Exceeds Standards
3   Meets Standards
2   Approaching Standards
1   Below Standards
0   Nonexistent

I.   Organization/Structure of the Essay   Yes/No
A. Thesis: Does the thesis take a firm position on the essay topic?   _____
B. Topic Sentences: Do topic sentences strongly support the thesis?   _____
C. Conclusion: Does the conclusion persuasively affirm the thesis?   _____
    Score: _____

II   Evidence: Part I — Accuracy and Adequacy of Evidence
A. Accuracy: Is all evidence accurate (true)?   _____
B. Adequacy: Is enough evidence used?   _____
    Score: _____

III   Evidence: Part II — Validity and Persuasiveness of Evidence
B. Validity: Do explanations of evidence make sense?   _____
A. Persuasiveness: Do explanations of evidence support main ideas?   _____
    Score: _____

IV   Language Mechanics
A. Punctuation: Does the essay use correct punctuation?   _____
B. Grammar: Does the essay use correct grammar (sentence structure)?   _____
C. Spelling: Is spelling correct?   _____
    Score: _____

V   Writing Process
A. Prewriting: Are all prewriting activities complete?   _____
B. Effort: Is great effort shown in these activities?   _____
    Score: _____

Total Score: _____ X 5 = Grade: _____

Copyright © by John De Gree 2006. All rights reserved

Made in the USA
Columbia, SC
15 June 2021